2.75
28¢

*Also by Robert Hillyer*

### RIVERHEAD
( 1932, out of print )
A Novel

### COLLECTED VERSE
( 1933 )
Winner of the Pulitzer Prize for 1934

### A LETTER TO ROBERT FROST AND OTHERS
· ( 1937, out of print )
Satirical Epistles in Heroic Couplets

### PATTERN OF A DAY
( 1940 )
Lyrics and Satiric Pieces

### POEMS FOR MUSIC, 1917-1948
( 1949 )
Lyrics

*These are Borzoi Books,*
*published in New York by Alfred A. Knopf*

# THE DEATH OF CAPTAIN NEMO

# The Death
# of Captain Nemo

A NARRATIVE POEM

BY

ROBERT HILLYER

ALFRED A. KNOPF NEW YORK 1949

THIS IS A BORZOI BOOK,
PUBLISHED BY ALFRED A. KNOPF, INC.

FIRST EDITION

TO

*VIRGINIA KENT CUMMINS*

# *The Argument of the Poem*

CAPTAIN NEMO, his submarine yacht, and the oceanic grotto on the volcanic isle are familiar to the reader from the pages of Jules Verne's *Mysterious Island*. There is no further similarity between Verne's excellent fantasy and the present work.

The time of the action is three days in the autumn of 1945. Two war-weary American poet-sailors are navigating their sloop to the East Indies. They have stopped off at the volcanic island where Nemo's submarine is moored. The poem opens on the day of his death at the age of almost a hundred.

The first section of the poem serves as an overture. The next six sections trace a fragmentary account of Nemo's life through passages from his Journal: his fatherless boyhood in the little chateau by the river Cher in Touraine; his dreams of wealth based on an ancestral chart showing a Spanish treasure ship; his exiles and travels; his meeting with a nihilist involved in the assassination of Alexander II of Russia; and, after the Franco-Prussian War of 1870, his conviction that the decline of European civilization that began with the French Revolution will continue to the end. Despairing of peace, he locates the treasure ship, and, thus enriched, constructs his submarine yacht, the *Nautilus*.

The guiding love of his life is a lady he refers to merely as the Princess. His physical encounters with a peasant girl end in ironic disillusionment. For some years he is under the malign influence of a woman of occult powers whom he calls the Witch. These figures, rising from the pages of the old Journal, haunt the thoughts of the two young sailors.

In the eighth section, the two sailors, according to Nemo's instructions, sink the *Nautilus* with Nemo's body lying in state in the main cabin. Thereafter the volcanic island explodes, and the young men set forth in their sloop.

The ninth and last section, until the very end, is a monologue by one of the sailors as he lies on deck while his companion is asleep below. At the end he is aroused from his revery by the companion.

# THE DEATH OF CAPTAIN NEMO

# I

In the festooned cave, the vault half undersea,
O sea nymphs garlanded with seaweed, weaving
Your watery paces among white stalactites,
Weave also now your song. Make with your music
The fields of sunlight. Sing *La Beauce en fleur*
And the brown vintners plucking the grapes of Time.
Sing of the rivers, the Cher rippling beneath
Gray arches, Diane de Poictier's Chenonceaux,
Where the cold, hooded hearths gape open skyward,
And salamanders keep their unwinking watch
Among the ashes of long burnt-out loves;
And by St. Avertin rippling where willows
Whisper beneath the drooping moon a hint
Of dying and of grace; sing of the Loing
That murmurs words the shadowy canals
Have lost in centuries of silence under
The dark forest of Fontainebleau. Sing boyhood
In that lost land.
                    For the old man lies dying.

In the festooned cave, the vault half undersea,
Sea nymphs among the stony moss and intricate

Stone roses, wind-flowers, pale anemones
That bloom for ever; sweetly singing nymphs
Weave with your music the bright fields of sunlight
While he lies dying in the far-traveled vessel,
The harmless submarine, which in the depths
Wound like a thought in a philosopher's mind
Among the crypts of everlasting change,
Until it came to rest in the watery grotto
On the volcanic island. The low arch
Of the grotto, framed in halted floods of lava,
Rumbled to the sluggish tide while the boat came gliding
In, far in, to the uttermost midnight mooring
And anchored dimly glowing, as last thoughts dimly
Glowing fade in caves of a midnight brain.
Soon he will travel again down rivers rippling
Among the willows, to sink away in grace.

Lure him in sweet delirium; the dying
Brain flickers with phosphorous beauty: boyhood
Bounding uphill to a grove of twittering aspens,
Where from the top he looks to another summit,
And beyond to another where beyond lies Paris,
The Princess, the Court Ball, the theater curtain
Rising to show a ballet by Delibes;
Then as the swan flies, as we measure distance
Between the song and death, a flight of clouds
Wings over weather warnings, darkens all,
*Exeunt omnes.*

In his later years
He had an organ on his boat, the *Nautilus,*
And played the black keys only, giving, it is said,

4

## Captain Nemo

A Scottish melancholy to his music,
When his autonomous fingers still remembered
The thoughts that mind had sealed and heart had frozen
In amber to benumb the sting: wan battles,
Collapsing palaces, hysterical women
Torn from the pages of Euripides;
Boyhood betrayed; youth maimed; love, loyalty, murdered;
Chaos roaring above the calls for peace,
Till, with no backward glance lest hope betray him,
He dived deep down.

                But what are these dreams of dreams?
These memoirs of a life he never lived?
Where was the land where no one had a name?
In most familiar confidence he was
Most reticent. All was anonymous.
The long life's code, deciphered in his heart,
Came from his lips like mediæval Latin
Illuminated with so intricate flowers,
All scrolled, all golden, and the letter lost.
And yet his undersong was gay, a half-heard
Harpsichord beneath the organ music,
More French than Scotch, more Renaissance than either,
Elizabethan Renaissance, perhaps,
The Gothic vault sealed with the Tudor rose.

Most mothered man, who had never known a father
Except as a bugle call by a long-closed grave
When the white daisies shone like daytime stars
Beside the river solemn beneath the willows,
Telemachus he was, yet no one told him
His father's tale of Ilium and the Isles.

Seeking his father he came to his life's close
Far off from all emotion except one:
Pity, a cold pity, devoid of tears.
But if his heart was empty, consider the riches
Stored in the foundering brain.

                                      The old man stirs.
He sighs, the living glow goes out of his hands
Waxlike along the sheet, like the waxen hands
Of the mechanic chess-player worked with wires
By an old champion hidden among the draperies
And guiding the play in mirrors, long ago
In the famed Eden Musée. Consider the learning
Lost in this death, the music stored in the nerves;
The languages, long Latin, fibrous Greek,
And modern tongues in the minor key of love,
The nightingale singing by cloudy tides —
What was the use of the years shaping experience
Stored in so perishable a coffer? Why
These exquisite manners so unmannerly ended?
Grief will not rain on this so fertile death
The tears that water sapless blooms of ghost-land:
Pale wreaths that, when the mourners all are gone,
Stand fingering the air at dusk to frighten
The children amid the scuff of fallen leaves
And bonfire smoke. For this death only pity
Shines down like one star too far off for naming.

Now the last breath pencils the flaring nostrils.
The jaw drops. The eyes go out like sparks.

6

# II

"Gravely I say to you, my mother, you have
Deserted me upon this Norman hill.
I am a foundling left at my own doorstep,
The foster-parent of my childhood, old
Before my time. I sit and watch the ships
Outbound against the dazzling afternoon
And say, 'Whatever I have wished to do
Must be postponed.' Some other incarnation
More fortunate will set me in the picture
That hangs beneath the sky, the bright confusion
Framed in its frame of sunlight, showing less
Of earth's intent than man's diversity,
And both somewhat obscured by the beholder."

Shall I read on? The notebook is not private.
The dead have nothing private but their tombs:
Have I not held the south wind in my hands,
And worn the heart of John Keats on my sleeve?
Come now, I'll read this manuscript — you, too,
Over my shoulder. Ghosts do not walk these years.

"More man's intent than earth's diversity."

7

The line has changed. I did not read it so
One moment thence. Words, meanings, manuscript,
All, if we do not watch with jailer's eyes,
Slip from their meanings and reverse their tracks.
Begin again:

       "Truly, my father, you have
Left me a chart showing where treasures lie
But marked no compass points. The galleon sank
In a lagoon to windward of the reef;
Your grandfather had it from his grandfather,
But whence the wind came that soft afternoon,
Which way the wavelets over the sharp coral
Were ruffled, no man knows. The parchment served
To mystify my boyhood, and a sonnet
I scrawled along the margin won my first love
Among the formal bric-a-brac she cherished
More than her dainty husband. 'Break his heart?
What nonsense! Careful there, that Sèvres medallion.'

"How many volumes of the lives I've noticed
Are stacked unwritten on the shelves. By moonlight
I take them down and read. As a child seeing
His first play shouts a warning to the hero,
So, in the spectral light, turning the pages,
I would unwind the past and wind it up
Another way: 'Do not wait there, dear Charles,
Just at the bottom of the stairs at tea-time;
You'll hear that witty friend telling your wife
Some reconstructed half-truth from your past.
Move out of earshot, just a yard or two,
And you and she will walk in linked contentment

Always; she does not mind; she will forget
Unless — ah, it's too late: the mad denial!'

"So have I walked about a vanished landscape
And rearranged the accidents, yet knowing
All was inevitable, if not then
And by those means, still by some other flaw
Picked at by fate until it cracked the heart,
And, perhaps worse, the noble bric-a-brac.

"With confidence, I could have been an artist,
But the age I inhabited said No;
Or walking in the wood I might have followed
Arthurian roads that end by a wild seashore
Where, when death struck me, the assuaging barge
With the three dolorous queens would bear me westward
Unto that other island, where no earthly
Treasure lay, but the triune peace of God.
Now, with my chart in hand, I turn away
From prospect of such poverty, compute
Pacific miles, provisions, cost and hazard:
The galleon lies in one of five lagoons
To windward of the reef. With so much gold
I can outbuild the chateaux of the Loire,
Move in a caliph's dream from hall to hall
Where lamps and perfumes hanging in the gloom
Vie with each other's softness till the eyes
Breathe sweetness, and the nostrils feast on color;
Where love dares not speak openly of age,
Nor even mirrors sharpen to the truth.
It lies to windward. Which way blew the wind
That August day three hundred years ago?"

9

Here let us pause and light a cigarette.
The question's answered by the circumstances.
Whatever was to be found, the old man found it,
But somehow, affluence did not please; perhaps
His audience was not worthy of his splendor,
Or else the clutter of magnificence,
That makes a man accessory to things,
Palled on him. Nothing but a treasure ship
Weighed down with Indian wealth could have arisen
So phoenix-like more glittering than itself
As this deep-diving yacht is to the galleon.
Here float the chateaux packed into one vessel,
One hermitage, and soon (we'll not deny him
His final word) sarcophagus of light
It will go down unfathomably, fading
From glare to glow to glimmer and to blackness.
So sink ambitions, even solitudes
That in the end are more vainglorious
Than all the ambitious glories of the world.

"Euripides saw Athens sail away
From the Piræus, watched Alcibiades,
No longer young, but plump, and with thin hair
And too long mimicry of boyhood, urge
Athenian youth as it embarked for ever
For Syracuse, the fever-haunted marshlands
Of Sicily, whence no more they should come
Unless their ghosts along the rotting wharves
Weep as they ask each other, 'Where is Athens?'
Well may the ghost of Athens ask where they are,
With spent eyes gazing ever out to sea.

"At midnight, I who write this fled Sédan
And saw the Germans on their way toward Paris.
I thought how Aristotle taught one conqueror
To deal more gently than a conqueror would
With worlds that clasp his feet. But this is no
Aristotelian mind, not Alexander,
But someone else, some conqueror from the steppes.

"Princess, the curtain does not fall, but see
The stage is empty; they have all departed,
The dancers and the music. May I go?
I would surmise the Orient is upon us;
Not Buddha, not Confucius, Lao Tze,
But Genghis Khan with all his commissars.
Princess, we are in the wrong part of the city:
Take my advice, don't try to reach your home
Tonight, wait here until another century,
Another incarnation. Meet me there."

# III

The old man lies in state. The candles burn
Bright in the cabin of the *Nautilus*.
His face is sharpened to a white denial
Of violence; it turns toward history.
Moscva, the mad musician of the island,
Plays organ voluntaries, while the candles
Slanting their light, play life across the features.
A heavy pall of purple velvet hangs
Behind him; in embroidered gold, thrice lettered,
*Nemo: Nemo: Nemo:* — Thrice Nobody.
What claim has zero on a number? void
On velvet, anonymity on name?
Or was the old man (for he had the pall
Prepared) jesting, or did he find a pattern
In three times Nemo where one made no rhyme?

The water in the cave, heavily breathing,
Gives but an oily hint of storm without,
Which can be seen stuffing the arch with darkness
Where the cave opens to the sea. Let us
Go face the storm. My heart amid such pallor

Fails; I have never learned to love the dead.
As if invoked by Virgil, swirling voices
Howl and shout and die away in wailing;
The breakers stamp down on the beach together
Making the island shudder; chaos racing
The wheeling globe wins to the westward, dragging
The night behind on streamers of torn cloud.
I have seen storms too many, wars too many;
Bring out the old notebook; we can find a shelter
In things long past under the yellow dune,
Where sand is piled like hours that have run out
In broken cones of time, where winds are still.

Who is the Princess? she is hard to follow
Drifting along these waves of faded writing
As though from Astolat.

         She was called Mathilde
Perhaps by error, for the name's erased,
And Blanche and Ruth — perhaps she had many names.
She was inscrutable, aloof, correct;
She would have graced a modern Court not often.
Here is her miniature, you see her face,
Eyes far apart, pale hair, and level brow;
You see the vanished gardens of Touraine
Where she would walk between the naked statues
A woman never to be thought of naked
Even in fantasy. She turns with half-smile
Acknowledging your bow, and so she passes
Down the clipped path, the colonnades of Love,
And where the lake laps on the marble wall
Steps down into her barge, is borne away

To dine with Flaubert in the lotus garden.
But there's no comedy in empty theaters;
The Princess, cloaked from head to foot, goes home
Alone, disdainful of the fear of thieves
That stalk the ill-lighted alleys. In her room
She yawns, flips pages of book after book,
Dante, Gaboriau, de Musset, Staël,
Goes over to the piano, strikes a note
Too loud for that thin night, and closes down
The instrument as though it were a coffin.
It is amazing how she puts off sleep
When there is nothing left to keep awake for;
All the suspense of something going to happen
Still teases her imagination though
It has no form; she is in love with nobody —
How the word echoes through the private room:
Nobody, nobody. Panic-stricken
She looks into her mirror to make sure
The one survivor of her world's still there.

All that is from the notebook. It goes on:
"Do you know Dürer's 'Knight, Death, and the Devil'?
I'll tell you whom the Knight is going to meet
When he turns off the road from Roncevaux:
It is his true love standing by the inn
Just at the goosegirl hour of twilight, when
The village pond is red with sunset embers.
She stands with arms akimbo, shrewdly blooming,
And every charm complete with counter-charm
For quick reversal when his whims reverse.
Her laughter shocks him and he reins his horse.

'Do you love music, doxie?' 'O, I am
Most skilled in music.' 'And do you play chess?'
'I am the champion of three counties.' 'Are you
Faithful in love?' 'That can I vouch for, surely,
Having loved none but you. I saw you pass
Once with your friends across the bridge. I saw you
Once with the Princess.' She observes the frown
And so defies it. 'A most pallid woman,
The Princess; better blood flows in my veins
As running brooks are better than still ponds.
I see that you are melancholy-laden
With armor on your heart. Be pleased to drop it;
Safe in my bed your heart needs no protection.
That helmet, too: ah, why should thought so shining
Be nullified behind lack-luster gold?'

"Then from the hills the Witch summoned me back.
I, who loved Paris, and could bathe more coolly
In dust that sang of the Ægean Sea
Than with a rout of mermaids at Ostend,
Half-Greek, half-modern, I was snared like rhyme
In a refrain by mediæval minstrels:
'The Princess and the Goosegirl and the Witch.'
There is a notion that with railway trains,
Rifles and stock exchanges and republics,
Magic, both black and white, was sterilized
By caustic fact. Ah, but the sidelong glances
The stars in passing through the streets of night
Cast on this rustic earth do so beguile him
With Babylonian longings, ancient arts
Of love, that in the seventh house of heaven

The wine cups made of skulls clank round together
As the old toast is drunk among the dice.
For seven years she held my soul in thrall,
The enchantress of green night and feathery trees.
Where balm of Gilead perfumed the air
And the new moon drenched all the sedge with dew
She taught me loveless love that made me wan
At thought of mortal woman. I have heard
That after I had served my seven years
They captured her afar from her charmed circle,
Shriveled and snarling, and they trussed her up,
Impaled her heart, buried her at the crossroads,
And beat the ground down with the sign of the Cross
But when the wind is from a charnel quarter
And wisps of pale cloud fret the evening sky,
On upland roads in her abandoned country,
'Nemo!' I hear her whisper, and her shroud
Flutters and rustles in the rising wind.

"Here I left off three years ago. Meanwhile
Another war has harvested this village,
Leaving the chimney-stalks and husks of houses
With a few windows lighted this blue evening
Of cold December rain. Beneath my window
Two passersby go splashing down the highway.
I hear their voices: *Heureux Noël!*
How the great doors swing inward! Holy myth,
That flickers in the sanctuary lamp,
Still quaintly kindled and persistent myth
Where, having lost his way in darkness, Truth
Leans down and reads by reminiscent light
Directions homeward, and is reassured.

The little love god lying fast asleep
Does not observe what all about him see:
How wide and white the winter stars, how near,
While the huge earth goes swinging on through space
Like that (I watch one raindrop fall). Like that."

# IV

"The big white snowflakes sifting over Paris
Curve cupped in air like feathers of sea-birds,
Stipple the gray walls of the Louvre and wink out
On the black pavement. This bleak afternoon
The few who walk abroad, heads down, gloved hands
On hat-brims or upholding snug umbrellas,
Make haste toward home. But I am indecisive
And scan the lighted windows of my friends,
Wistful but not so pitiably lonely
As to mount stairways and assume my mask.
The Countess Jeanne McCarty in her salon
Welcomes yet younger poets as she ages
And underwrites their feuds. At Arthur's house
Malice lays waste the guests who are not there
Or take their leave too early. Henriette
Delights to sail half-way toward Cythera,
And there are others — praise the human heart! —
Whose goodness glows through clouds of stifled yawns.
In short, I miss the friends I never had.

"Through curiosity, as evening flowed
Between the misted lights of the shop windows,

18

I followed a small man clad all in black
Furtively down an alley where he wheeled
And beckoned me, and so we both descended
To a basement room, bare but for one scarred table
And one oil lamp which, as he turned it higher,
Showed his lewd mouth, flat nose, and slanted eyes.
'You are late,' he said, 'Czar Alexander's gone,
But where is Anarchy? Overruled as usual,
Just as we feared. The Czar is dead, long live —
Yet look!' and he unfolded an old map.
'Look here, and here.' Across five continents
His finger, the creased knuckles and black nail,
Moved steadily. It seemed that where he pointed
The names of cities disappeared, the boundaries
Melted together in a yellow smear
Spread over all the world. 'Can you foresee
The outcome and be patient as the mole
That blindly burrows down his tunnel knowing
By instinct when the turf is undermined?
My friend — But who are you? Who are you? You are
Not the one I expected. I have betrayed
My servants!' Quick my gaze pursued him. 'Gone,'
I said aloud, and as the lamp blew out
I was aware the window had no panes.
My warning is your warning."

There it stops,
And when we question Death, we hear time ticking.
For we are from another generation,
America, the country no one loves:
Whose people love all countries but their own,
Despising what they grasp. See how tiaras

Regret they are not twinkling on a peeress
In English boredom at an English court,
How women stir beneath importunate lovers
Yearning for France, how poets flee abroad
To cry *Ich Dien* among the ostrich plumes
And feed on boots, how mystic orators
Scream accusation from the slums, discerning
The lights of Paradise that gild the Kremlin;
While over all America fair fields
Are plowed in fury like the hapless women,
And then are blown away to hang in dust
A phantom map of farms no man would love
Down to the roots, and forests hacked and rotting
Rear sawdust mountains where the poisoned streams
Seek absolution from the indifferent sea.
It must be no one means to live there longer
Than parasites upon a dying host.
Holy America, who dreamed so well,
Folding her eastern over her western hand
In the slow clasp of peace, O it is time
For all her poets to come home again,
To claim her dreams from the retreating stars.

From here America and Europe both
Are dreams, and this volcanic isle still shaking
With birth, and we are dreamers who have found here
The epitome of a lost civilization
In this antique of France, philosopher
Whose own volcanoes, being long extinct,
Serene in snow-capped meditation rise
Above the kneeling sea.

Be careful there.
Only old men and nations should embrace
The Way of Quiet. Buddha and lotus looks
Walk strangely in our streets. Beneath his hand
The sky is lulled, but still I hear the surf
Pounding the outer reef, our pulse of the world.


No pulse, a ticking clock. What season is it?


Here or at home? There are no seasons here.
At home it is late autumn, autumn sunrise,
Filtered through haze and fiery colored leaves,
And on the sea it dazzles where the dories
Loom up half visible, and voices carry
Over the tide and gurgle of green shells
Along the ebbing flats.

                Those are but symbols
Of homesickness, and if we drank a bottle
We soon could weep. But truly, every day
We saw them without seeing them. The dead
Must suffer thinking how they took for granted
The small things never to be found again,
Not through eternity. Do they remember?
Do distant reed-notes from our fields pursue them
With music of regret for long days wasted
And loyal love spurned?

               I flip these mildewed pages
And find young Nemo knew the same despair:

"The words 'Farewell, Princess' were on my lips.
We stood surrounded by departing guests
Noisy with weariness. She wrung my hand
And drew me to one side. 'As you have said,
We shall await another incarnation,
And yet I go with you, you stay with me,
You in my book of hours and I in yours.'
The lights grew blurred among the girandoles
And the huge shadows swayed from side to side
As I went down the stairs alone to darkness.

"Months after that, one green night on the desert
When the white stars like daisies in the grass
Seemed near enough to gather, I recalled
The seeress Diotima and her words
To Socrates. (A wandering man who loves
His books must make his mind a library:
Then he can read by starlight.) Diotima
Having described the love beyond desire
For mortal youth, revealed the ultimate love
That fastening on none, seeks out in all things
Whatever part of beauty may be found,
Till from so many fragments to the last
Secreted spark, the many shine as One.

"Then suddenly I shivered, I was aware
Of the long, never-traveled road toward home.
And with my eyes still on the starlit page
Of memory, I read from that same discourse
How Aristophanes conversed on love:
In the beginning of the world our souls
Were split in two, and through all life thereafter

22

Each half goes looking for the other half
And questions every gaze, 'Are you my lover?'
And that idea of half-souls, of reunion,
Moved me to think how one half was the man,
The other half his native country. Only
The exile knows the pangs ascribed to love.

"This desert where I yearn for France was green
Four thousand years ago. The lost Egyptian
Exiled from here cried to the homing birds,
'Is no one left who speaks the tongue of Egypt?'
And the Chinese poet, sent to a far province,
Thought of his friends and wept. 'In this dull place
There is no one to be called remotely human.'
By the waters of Babylon all men together
Sit down and weep. The many weep as One."

# V

"In the monastery where Fra Angelico
Left his indubitable and shining proof
Of courteous excursions into Heaven,
A young girl lingered past the hour of closing
And was pursued by grim custodians.
But she had come three thousand miles to witness
The Coronation of Our Lady; wherefore
She fled up the dim stairs. In failing light
The Glory gave its own light. God the Father
Held out the clustered stars to God the Son
Chosen to crown His Mother; in the air
The Holy Ghost hushed Heaven with hovering wings.
In that suspended moment the guards entered
All clash and anger. But the girl escaped them.
The picture was in darkness. To this day
No one has noticed among kneeling saints
The half-hid figure of the shy newcomer.

"Was the rapt novice, lost to outer things,
Moved by devotion or by art to merge
Her own identity in what she worshiped?

24

Perhaps by both, like him, the saintly artist.
So pure a faith deserved a place in Heaven,
And let us grant her that rare miracle:
The union of these sundered aspirations
Toward God and Beauty in one flight of stairs.
Most rare, indeed, since first the Renaissance
Offered the homeless gods of Greece a shelter,
No honeyed-colored Parthenon, but ceilings
Whereon they could disport as amoretti
Blandly adorning art no longer Christian,
No longer anything but art for art,
As modern sensitives make fashionable
Discoveries of thrills left undefined
In Notre Dame de Chartres, thus condescending
Toward beauty of whose essence they know nothing.

"To be a Dante, one must know, like Dante,
The architecture of the many mansions
Down to the last entablature, and even
That knowledge waits on loftier truths beyond.
To comprehend a work that moves toward God
We had best start with God and work from Him
Who holds the key to labyrinths of art:
That is the highest criticism. Meanwhile,
When Beauty parts with God, religious people,
In shocked conclusion that all art is pagan,
Contrive such sanctuaries as would blight
All but the plaster saints with paper roses
Who simper round the dim confessionals.

"Why so much letter and so little spirit?
The gods of Greece had dignity enough

And wisdom to resent the blasphemies
Of aftercomers who missed all their meaning,
Their Pity and their Terror and their Peace.
From Egypt to the spire of Sainte Chapelle
All rose in piety, and every stone
Marked where some artist had invoked his god.
The Sainte Chapelle, stripped of its screen and altar
Means no more than so many walls and windows
Emptied of their intention, like poor Isis
Behind museum glass, her blank eyes fixed,
While the damp northern air dissolves the limestone
And grain by grain the goddess falls to sand.

"But the real Isis walked abroad one night
On the Egyptian desert; I could hear
Her childlike lamentation rise and fall:
'O Quiet Heart, where are you? O my brother!'
Not understanding gods who die, she faltered
Along the sands, calling her love, remembering
The dark head on the pillow, and around him
Among the plans but lately cast aside,
The fragments of his sacrificial body.
She still is heard, still unconsolable,
Among the dreams of women mourning soldiers,
And soldiers questioning everything they die for.
Think you that one of them was glad to die? —
Go ask the God who cried out from the Cross.

"To ward off evening chills of loneliness
The hermit warms his thought with indignation,
Casting old evils on the flames, yet knowing
How huge the forest looms whence come the faggots.

The fire grows hot, but all is a mirage
Where nothing can be done; we run in nightmares
And slip back with our speed.

                             A summons came
Across the desert: I could now return,
Not to my home, for that was sold, nor even
My homeland as I left it. Nothing remained
Of the old courtesy and grace of style
Which, since the people lacked them, they destroyed
Rather than take the trouble to acquire.
From windows of a gutted palace leaned
A row of harlots, chattering and drunken:
'See, now the poor enjoy the rich man's house!'
And in the street a child, clawing for food,
Examined solemnly a piece of canvas
Torn from a Titian; I could recognize
The master by his treatment of a hand,
One piece of the enormous picture-puzzle
Not to be reassembled in our time.

"I failed to find the Princess. She was gone,
Said one, to Amiens. She was not in Amiens;
To Tours, to Quiberon, to Avignon,
The length and breadth of France. Someone had seen her
In every village, or imagined so,
Or said so for my comfort. In the spring
I found myself walking by dim canals
Of Fontainebleau. One evening on the towpath
When all the country swam in misty green,
An alley of great trees stretched on before me
Like Dante and Virgil meeting overhead;

And at the tunnel's end the cooling sunset
Flared from a void framed by a Norman arch.
I laughed suddenly. Now there was nothing left.
Experienced, disappointed, mazed in learning,
I had at last, like one who rides all day
To find himself at evening where he started,
Alighted at the doorstep of my childhood,
Knowing with awe what any peasant knows:
'I am the Resurrection and the Life.'

"Ah, could the moment stay when all the tangled  ·
Strands are raveled out by holy skill
While the light shines! The archway quickly darkened
And down the dark went I, my instant lost
And not to be reclaimed. Though rise I will
At resurrection, I shall still be clad
In the gray cerecloth of philosophy,
An infant pupil in the lore of angels.
It has been said, 'The lips at Hallelujah
Long years of practice bore.' But not my lips."

# VI

Blessëd be islands when time comes to leave them!
In a few weeks we should have seen such things
As would have made unsuited to our fellows
Our everyday acceptance of the strange.
Last night I could have sworn I saw the Princess
Standing upon the beach as though she stood
Outside the theater waiting for her carriage,
Wan in the cloudlight of the drooping moon.
Her hair was smooth and glistered with small gems,
Her cloak was glimmering like a veiled cascade;
She stood so near, I could read *Oberon*
Upon the programme in her hand, and see
The sapphire ring she wore outside her glove.
This was her own dream she was standing in,
A phrase or two of Weber's on her lips;
To her I was not there, was yet unborn.
Just for a moment the subdued night noises
Of Paris in another age were with me:
The footsteps passing, tones of conversation,
The hushing leaves of unremembered summer,
The clop-clop, clop-clop of a horse's hooves
That stamped and shuffled to a restive halt.

I am still dizzy with nocturnal spinning
Against all time and gravity, back through
A century and half-way round the world,
Or else it was the world, not I, revolving.
If time and space are false, why then I'm bankrupt
Of all my natural wealth. Most beautiful
The Princess was, but dust should hold its own.

Perhaps she was some memory of Nemo's
Still hovering from his not yet frozen mind,
Like mists on cooling planets after sunset.
O, I was wakeful, too. Behind my hut
In the small wilderness of palms I saw
The vampire flushed with life-blood of the soul.
And yet what shakes me most is not the evil
But that I looked on it with natural candor,
As if to say, "There's something I have missed."
Wound up in witchcraft I reproached myself
For my long lack of ingenuity;
Something ineffable and foul leaped forth
From the last oubliette of my disdain.
And that's enough to say. I am quite myself,
Yet wiser, being kinder. Having found
Within myself these unacknowledged beings
I am well warned against all prejudice.

Nemo was more secretive in his writings
Than are these uninvited funeral guests.

Nemo and every man. Until last night
I did not know my tenants. Some I smile at
Passing on stairways, some steal in at night

To make a carnival of sleep, but these —
Now you are laughing. The whole thing is boyish
Almost to affectation. Yet it's true.

I am no doubter, but the crystal morning
Is all washed clean in penitence and tears;
I'm for reality when it's for me,
And the real world is good for the time being.
Tomorrow morning, then, farewell to Nemo
And to his wistful book. We'll leave it with him.

But pry a little more.

                We had been wiser
To start at the beginning and read through.
But listen: do you think he overheard me?

"We live in secret, Nemo and every man.
I am all men that live. I am your eyes
Who read these lines, yet am I Nobody.
Along the sliding stars from thought to thought
My being moves, yet when you see the starlight,
The star itself is æons on its way.
We live in forethought and in afterthought;
The present is a gaping void between.
All things are past before we know or feel them,
The keen blade cuts before the pain, we dwell
In memory, and that abyss between
Forethought and afterthought is not less deep
Than ages between us and Egypt, æons
Between the star and what we see of stars.
Forethought is the prediction of illusion,
Computing when the absent star will shine.

"When all computing's done, we reach that door,
Bronze, triple bronze to all the keys of science,
Where logic knocks with bloody knuckles raw,
And all philosophies claim keyhole views
Though no two make the same report; where faith
Waits for the host to swing the great doors wide
And knows that he will come. And he does come.

"Surely as all the rivers of the world,
Though they have various risings, various runnings,
And sometimes hide themselves far underground
Spreading in midnight lakes, but fall at last
Into the ocean, so after all our searchings,
Our curiosity and contemplation,
Man's reason ends, dissolving all its powers
In the necessity of Infinite power.

"Five hundred miles up the dense Orinoco
Yielded that single passage, and all else
Went drifting down between the jungles, waste
From undiscovered gold."

                    He traveled far.

What was the magnet?

                    The undiscovered gold?

He must have found that in the galleon — later.
Money and man seem never to agree
On the right time for meeting.

                              Give me money
And I'll arrange the happiest meeting.


                                        Yes,
So say the nations, and the battle's on.
To make the rich forget how poor they are
Makes others rich who furnish the diversions,
The wars, the concerts. Not much work is done
For natural need, food, shelter, clothing; mostly
We work to while away our apathy
And buy it back again, the price being life.

Is this the voice that told me of a morning
Washed clean in penitence and tears? Poor Nemo
Has squeezed your heart. Find me a livelier strain,
Timotheus.

            I can't foretell his pages:

"One thing we know of fate to each man's comfort
(And even the happiest man regrets some turning
On crossroads of his past itinerary):
Were we forevisioned with what every move
Would lead to, we would still from stubbornness
Or trust in luck or *deus ex machina,*
Go on in full view of the consequences.
What! will the maiden sour, grow foul, ill-humored,
Adulterous, deceitful, pandering
To my inferiors? I am as shrewd
As you; I also note the sprouting faults,
But love like mine can stagger prophecy,
Transmuting to some yet quiescent grace

                    33

Her lewder possibilities. She'll flower
To virtues unperceived by all your omens,
Needing but my desire to plant them there.

"I seem to hear young Nobody once more,
Pleading the goosegirl's virtue to the Princess,
Who, with clear sea-blue gaze looked out the window
Into the sky-blue calm, the steady sky,
The steady gaze, unclouded both. 'I hope
All that you say will be what you will say
Twenty years hence.' She smiled. 'Were I Cassandra,
Hector were dead before my eyes. You seem
Alive with love enough to keep Troy burning
A lifetime and yet never be consumed.'
I answered, 'You have learned to speak in riddles
Since my good fortune canceled our farewell.
Do you juggle symbols, poems à la mode?
Is this some idiom of the ateliers
Now that there is no Court?' 'I am not Cassandra
Nor Sappho nor the Sphinx. All I would say
Is simple, but it must be well concealed,
Something to be unwrapped when I am absent —
Years hence, perhaps. What are you asking for?
Do you know what you are asking for? My pride!'

"Years after, when her meaning was unwrapped
As she had said, and solitude at last
From shipwreck of my misadventured youth
Had salvaged wisdom and some gold, I told her
That now I understood. Was it too late?
Far-traveled and alone, I clenched the air
With lungs that breathed love's first full fiery breath.

34

Standing upon a cliff in Tierra del Fuego
To a dead woman I addressed my lovesong.
I write it now; I tell my future self,
However much doubt may bestride my view,
Once I saw clearly through the face of darkness
And looked into the face of light: My Love,
I have written prothalamions and sonnets
Each with its pleasurable fugue to hymn
The goddess and the harlot fleshed in one,
Dramatic scene, illusion, vanity,
To be dispelled by the least passing thought
Of how you twitched your veil before the mirror
Or poured the coffee. I once watched intent
While you drew on your glove, preoccupied
With the smooth fitting of each finger; then,
Spreading your hand, you looked up with a smile,
And we set out. It was a summer night,
The opera was Weber's *Oberon*.
Quite without warning, when the curtain fell,
You looked full in my face. 'If you don't love me,
Then I have wasted ten years of my life.'
And a perversity still unexplained
Froze me with panic. I said not one word.
The moment held its breath. You touched my arm:
'Please see me to the door and leave me there;
My carriage will be waiting.' 'Leave you there
Alone and unattended?' Ah, my Princess.
'Alone, perhaps. Attended by my thoughts
And by my servants. Isn't that enough?
Am I not lucky to have thoughts and servants?
Goodnight, dear friend.'
                            That is my song of love."

35

# VII

"In the hall of the house which I once called my own,
I stood with the wind, another trespasser.
It came through the doors that opened on the terrace
And brought along the sough of the sighing pines.
The house was empty; those who had bought it from me
Had wearied of dark pines that grew so tall
And the little lake that froze to winter silence
And chattered the summer away through the dripping culvert.
It was late March, the wind was wild but warm,
The house like a ship in heavy seas responded.
As I entered a shadowed room I saw on the door-frame
That stood out golden caught in a streak of sun
The pencil lines that marked the growth of a child,
Each year the height and date scratched in the woodwork,
And then I knew that my heart would never break.
I looked down from a window: all was gone
In a waste of weeds, the vineyard, the rose-garden;
So I turned from the house with freedom and relief,
No longer the custodian of decay.
I was satisfied; there was nothing more to do;
I must go from there and this time go for ever.

_The Death of Captain Nemo_

"In Brest I discovered a ketch, the _Antoinette,_
She had been a fisherman and then a yacht;
Now in the gay green sunlight painters and carpenters
With song and blasphemy renewed her youth.
Paint-brushes slapped her sides, hammers clanged over
The bay and echoed against surprised gray houses
That stood on stilts in the wash of the little inlet.
The _Antoinette_ should become my privateer
With letters of marque to chase to the farthest horizon
That rakish vessel _Contentment_ and make her my prize.
I had a crew of five, excellent Bretons,
Who hated everything, and themselves included,
But most of all the sea, who fawned upon them
The while she lay in wait to drown her lovers.

"My _Antoinette_ was solid, and she sat
Plumply upon the water like a swan,
And like a swan's neck her most gracious bow
Curved to the bowsprit. _Splendor_ is the word
For any ship we love. A sailor knows
My ship already, and one who does not know
Would but become entangled in the rigging
Of my description. Let him see her then,
A black, two-masted vessel leaning taut
Along the wind, close-hauled with gleaming sails,
The blue sea cresting white each side her prow,
And sea-gulls balancing the composition —
Is that the way to paint sea-pictures? Follow
Her course eight months; the sails become moth-color,
The black hull whitens with the brine, her speed
Slackens with drag of barnacles; and see,
In the expanse of watery Sahara

Where pallid clouds unmoving as the Sphinx
On the opaque horizon loom for days,
She lies becalmed, slow-heaving with the swell,
While the storm lurks accumulating fury.

"One afternoon a cold front menacing
As doom and laced with intermittent lightning,
Moved in across the sea, hung just above us,
Then thundered down like coal. We met with rage
The charging mountains and the purple wind.
They ripped our reefed-down mainsail while the ketch
Baring her teeth rose screaming to confront them.
We set a trysail, held her to the wind
And as the bow climbed up each murderous slope
I eased her off a little over one crest
To meet the next because we had to meet it,
Although each seemed the last. But *Antoinette*
Was fighting, the old forest in her timbers
Roared, cracked like cannon, threshed and shrieked aloud
Hatred to hatred, remembering old scores.
The sailors cursed the ship, the sea, and God,
And most of all cursed me, shaking their fists
As we surmounted one wave after another.
Yet, when the stormsail went, they had a second
Rigged and in place, bent like a pistol shot,
And every groaning line held to its utmost
Watched by ten Druid eyes. At last as night
Swirled down upon us and the storm redoubled
Maniacal, blind force, those seamen knew
Just at what instant by one hair of balance
I was to be relieved. One took the helm
Transferring from my tension to his own

With gradual hold the uninterrupted course,
And as I went below, the little ship
Fought on, her shoulders braced by Breton fury.

"Lying in darkness, up I mounted, up
Laboriously, lurched from side to side,
Then dropped as though the ship came down on rock
To grind and shudder there; then up once more,
The straining climb, and all my bones became
The framework of the ship, wrenched, pulled, and pounded,
My teeth set, and I wondered just how long
The contest could go on. The sea slid hissing
Along the sides three inches from my hand,
And underneath bilge water to and fro
Sloshed in the well; the mast creaked in its step,
And overhead on deck big clumping boots
Stamped as though coming through. I think the hatred
Which made the Bretons masters of the storm
Came from their Druid forebears. The mad Vikings,
Seafolk for ever, fared forth with a shout;
The stocky Bretons thought of Druid temples
When they built ships, and with a forest curse
Repulsed wild winds and waves with magic wood.
In that Pacific wilderness I saw
A dolmen standing stark against the wind
On a wide plain rain-lashed and tenantless
In Brittany twelve thousand miles away."

Here he breaks off, and the next entry finds him
In China.

How long after?

He doesn't say.
This is all piecemeal. Ah yes, here's the story
Written in retrospect: the typhoon wearied
Before the ship did; three days later found them
At anchor by an island, and he says:

"Since from the whole expanse of the Pacific
We had arrived at Somewhere long familiar
On an old yellow parchment, I conclude
That Someone had predestined us for Somewhere,
And the typhoon itself took on new meaning.
There were the five lagoons, concentric arcs
Within five reefs cradling the tiny island
With one small topknot of disheartened palms
That leaned one way from the prevailing wind.
To one side of them stood a single wall
Of what had been a fortress built of coral
And on a point a gallows-looking crosstree
From which, suspended like a tavern sign,
A metal plaque, bearing a coat of arms,
Creaked back and forth perpetually ill at ease.
We anchored off the island, went ashore
And from a basin of rainwater filled
Our few remaining casks. No one was there
Or had been there for indeterminate years.
The wind was steady from the east-southeast
And blew the heat out of the golden sunlight.
All the palms slanted from the east-southeast:
'It lies to windward.' East-southeast was windward
That August day three hundred years ago.
And there to windward lay in clear shoal water
A galleon all of coral, hull and spars,

Perfect enough to be a coral brooch
Shaped for the necklace of some giant woman.
Skeleton white it was with roseate shadows
Where the portholes had been and coral shafts
Where once had been the guns. My crew and I
Stared at the stony ship and crossed ourselves:
We feared there might be coral men below.
Barnacles first, I thought, to ossify
The wood and even the heavier shrouds and ratlines,
And then on barnacle foundation, coral,
To weld His Catholic Majesty's ambition
Into world history as the planet writes it.

"No doubt he would have been more gratified
To lay up treasure in a handier vault,
Yet he gained much in Heaven: before leaving
With all that long-sequestered wealth, we offered
Prayers for his soul, and probably the first.
We sailed for China, landed at Foochow,
And there divided share and share alike,
Which, with the gift of *Antoinette,* brought out
More sun than ever shone on Brittany
From the five smiling faces of my friends.
They still were waving as they sailed from sight,
And maybe set a watch to go on waving
All the way overseas to Brittany,
Where, knowing *Antoinette* and seamanship,
I am quite sure they landed in due season.
Nor would they care what government the landsmen
Had set up as a scarecrow in their absence;
If they disliked new masters and new taxes
Or latest rats elected from the sewers,

There lay the *Antoinette* at anchor, there
Beyond all government the sea arranged
Pale sunset panoramas of delight.
They knew — as now I know — the only free man
Remains the one who never comes ashore.

"Yet who would choose vagaries of the ocean
Except in preference to those of men?
To escape all tyrannies there lie black fathoms
Where tempest can not pierce nor passion brew
Its visible calamities. A sage
Whom I discovered by a waterfall
Counting the colors in the arch of spray
Through centuries while emperors reigned and died,
Gave me a word to secret artisans
Who were his clan along the northern seaboard.
T'ang was their name. They could lay out a landscape
Of Heaven inside an agate stone, arranged
To fade out in the shadow and appear
Once more in sunlight; on the gnat-wing bridge
The tiny people bowed with folded fans
And smiled with sunlight greetings as though weather
Were chance instead of a huge hovering hand.
The T'angs delighted to outdo inventions
That held the West in awe, and with contempt
Break up the things as soon as they devised them.
'And them it was the Son of Heaven called
To his imperial footstool when he needed
Their skill to chide a foolish Saxon Queen.
She gave him, to display her people's craft,
One fine steel needle, symbol of her strength
Tempered with delicacy. For three years

The clan of T'ang worked on the foreign thing,
And for three years the Son of Heaven labored
Shaping a poem. These are the sacred words:
*Her cherished gift, steel needle fine and tempered,*
*The Queen bestowed upon the Son of Heaven,*
*Who with these lines returns the gift as worthy*
*Only of her who sent it. May she always*
*Deign to examine hidden truths in things.*
*Surely the needle is of steel, yet draws*
*A golden thought,* the Emperor wrote. Inside
That needle the T'angs cunningly had shaped
Twelve smaller needles, each within the other,
A nest of needles growing ever finer
So that the last was hardly to be seen.
These are the artisans to build your *Nautilus;*
I have summoned the image to their minds already.'

"In later days I wondered as I cruised
Among blind creatures in the crypt of being
And prowled the dead streets of Atlantis, whether
This everlastingly nocturnal roamer
Was really I, Nemo, or if the rainbow
That hangs in permanent illusion over
The roaring gorge of time beholds two sages,
Old T'ang and Nemo with another name.

"In what past would you like to lose yourself?
For you may choose some day when all is spread
Beneath you, the green labyrinth whose paths
Mazed you from birth to death. Some day you will sit
Above them and examine the whole tangle,
Wrong turns, false exits, tricks that made you laugh

43

When you were young and all day lay ahead,
Then frightened you, then wearied you to death
As expectation failed, and night, too near,
Discredited all dreams that made you young.
Your pasts will all be spread beneath you, peopled
Just as they were, the settings all in place,
And here and there you'll choose an episode
That once seemed happy, but as knowledge dawns
That though you may repeat you can not alter
One grassblade, one mistake, one consequence,
You will have had enough: 'Come, little Jacques,
Stand by the doorframe and I'll measure you.
Don't push up taller. There, I'll make the mark.
Two inches and a half in one short year!
And think of all the years to come!' The pines
Sigh in the rising wind. You have had enough.
It is time to try a new life somewhere else,
Perhaps to fail again, but not so hugely;
Or if as hugely, in a new adventure;
Or if the old one, you will never know."

# VIII

All ready, there?

        *All ready, there?*

                Hear Echo.

*Hear Echo!*

        Answer, Echo.

            *Echo, Echo.*

Harken, she answers cavern after cavern
Between the water and reverberant walls.

Be satisfied, and let poor Echo rest
And set a good example to old Logos
Who talks back to Himself among the planets
Shaking reluctant syllables of life
That clung like bats of silence to the cave
Till He dislodged them scolding into sunshine,
Half-blind and wholly inarticulate.

45

But listen!

        Yes, I have listened this half hour:
It is the drip of water from stalactites
Into the ebbing tide, like a clock ticking
Or bells ringing or a thousand other sounds
Liquid and mournful.

        No, there is something else,
Some deep uneasiness among the roots
Of this volcanic isle.

        Come now, it's time.
Get in the dinghy, we have work to do
Aboard the *Nautilus,* close up the hatches,
Turn all the lights on, open the sea-cocks,
And let the dazzling catafalque descend.

You have the little book?

        Here in my pocket.
Years hence we doubtless will regret the scruples
That made us give it back to him.

        Years past,
We would have been too scrupulous to read
One page of it.

        I read it all last night.
These disconnected episodes assume
A shape from which I learned what I'd unlearn
Had I the proper drug. We live at once

46

In simultaneous time unnumbered lives
That in the flash of our immortal moment
Spring to one unified design; we are
Like islands seemingly divided, yet
All part of one vast Asia undersea.
I tell you, the whole universe is only
One flash. Let there be light, and there was light.
One flash in darkness. By my thought of this
I master it. Some other time I'll tell you,
Now's not the time: that saying works both ways.
Here, take the painter, make it fast right there
On that convenient cleat. She may go down
Much sooner than the old man thought she would,
And I'm for safety.

            Don't forget the wine
He wanted us to drink to his farewell.
How still it is down here, how very still.

It's strange to find him lying as we left him,
Each finger curved in place, the mouth so final,
The angle of each separate hair the same.
Perhaps the face is sharper. One who loved him
Should have been here.

            There is no one left who loved him.
I'll wind the clock up, that will last a month.
You think the water will not flood this cabin?

No, on the word of all the T'angs it won't.
He will lie here as long as any trace
Of Nemo can avoid eventual dust,
And for a month the clock will tick and chime

47

To keep him company, hours warding off
Eternity a while in case he's lonely.

The clock will be the lonely one. Nemo
Has done with time. He is so far from here
He does not see me as I fill these glasses
And hand you yours and pick mine up and say:
"Farewell, we leave you with eternal friends."

This is a vintage from his childhood chateau
Beside the river Cher, you see the picture
There on the bureau, a sweet place it was
Among the vineyards.

      When these grapes were ripe
Charles X was on the throne of France, since when
France has not had a throne worth speaking of.

They are very proud of that.

        Give me your glass.
Speak of his happiness. What of his boyhood?
What of his childhood days?

       He had a friend,
A young Chevalier nameless like the others,
And from their boyhood till the time when love
Gravely divides young men for women's pleasure,
They breathed one air, together climbed the Alps,
Sailed for a year across Phœnician fields,
Shared prizes for their Greek hexameters,
And loved the image each saw of the other
In the first girl they kissed. Those days were happy.

Even in those days cobwebs on this bottle
Were filming it with years. The eloquent wine
Speaks after man is silent.

                        Happiness?
Yes, in that boyhood friendship. After boyhood
Happiness grew more complicated, dwelling
In expectation. It was happiness
No doubt, that kept him hovering round the Princess, —
She was unhappy that he shunned the flame.
She has been dead these many years, she died
Before his visit to his ancient home;
He scarcely mentioned it. "I shall not see
Except in fading memory, the dear Princess.
I recommend her to St. Chrysostom."
The goosegirl was more durable than that:
She got a poet in trouble, married him,
Took him to Paris, and having climbed as far
As literature would take her, clambered through
The bedroom window of an Irish earl
And kicked the ladder out from under her.
As Countess Jeanne she held her court in Paris
Just at a time when mercifully for her
Bad language and coarse manners were in vogue.
Immortal girl, she can not die.

                        A smile
Flickered the old man's face.

                        He knew his world.
Here — one more glass apiece and there's an end.
Our sloop is ready; long before you wakened

I went aboard and stowed our gear below.
And by tomorrow at this time we'll be,
With luck, well on our way toward Celebes.

Shall we close down the coffin?

                          As you will —
No, there's no reason to. Let him lie there,
There may be other mourners than ourselves
Whose presence we are unaware of, waiting.
Ah, here's the handle. With one twist the sea-cocks
Open just wide enough to let her down
Slowly, with dignity. Are all the lights on?

Gleaming from stem to stern.

                        All ready, then.
You hear that hissing? That's the air forced up
By water seeping in. On deck, my friend,
The *Nautilus* is sinking under our feet.
Get in, I'll row; you sit in the sternsheets,
I'm heading for that shelf of shaly rock,
An excellent point of vantage. Are you weeping?
Then I'll not hide my face.

                    The deck's awash now.
The amber lights evaporate through water,
Melting like moonlight in a wash of cloud.
Down, down they go, dimmer, now they are gone.
How dark the darkness.

                  Give me your hand. What's that,
That clang?

*Captain Nemo*

The rock seems shifting underfoot.
Feel it? The whole foundation's shuddering.

One long wave swirled along the surface. Hurry,
We must get out of here, the grotto's crumbling.
Quick or the entrance will be blocked. Come out!

No, but we mustn't leave the rowboat here,
We'll need it. Take the painter, I'll fend off
While you tow.

It's like running in a dream.

But we have gained the arch. The sun is hanging
Burly and bloated through a veil of smoke.

Dark purple background and the red-hot mountain
Like Fujiyama painted in bright blood
Against the night.

I'll look when I'm aboard.
Easy, just bring us up under her stern.
Now I feel safe again. Haul on the anchor,
I'll hoist the mainsail. Just in time, my friend;
Five minutes later would have been too late.

There's a fair wind to bear us out of range.
Volcanoes should remember they're extinct;
They're more convulsive than old men in love.

And more impressive. What a pyre for Nemo!
He'll think he's pulled the whole world after him.

51

The island is a giant of itself,
A lump of bulging smoke feathered with flames.
Huge bursts of slag and rubble blaze sky-high
Trailing their smoke.

    The wind is dying out.
I am afraid we've not come far enough
For safety. Over there beneath the smoke
The ocean boils with white-hot lava; listen,
I hear the hiss of the indignant tide
And a wild wail — what is it? — like the hoot
Of staring owls among the cosmic rafters.
I am afraid.

   The wind holds, faint but steady.
We'll make it.

    The whole mountain's going up!
It's cracked from top to bottom, one vast coal
Splitting in two, the core of flame exposed
And raging. The whole mountain's split in two!
Stop up your ears! Put your hand over your face!

The sloop with dreamlike gentleness climbs up
An earthquake wave as tall as the collapsing
Heights that thundered splashing into the sea.
And now, as gently setting down the sloop,
The earthquake wave goes onward bound for Asia,
Gliding over the sea, it leaves us rocking
With the faint wind slatting our idle sails,
Fanning the night, fanning the empty night.

# IX

You are a poet sitting in a garden
One afternoon with summer in your hair,
The Queen of England paces down the pathway
And smiles and stops to ask you for a rhyme.
She too is writing poetry, a sonnet
To speed unwelcome princes from her strand.
And royal policies through rhymed iambics
Can best conceal the purpose of her whim.
The Queen goes on, the poet shrugs his shoulders,
The interruption is a good excuse
For doing nothing but survey the garden
With summer wind and sunlight in his hair.
That was another Queen, another poet,
The Thames was silver and the age was gold;
Perhaps the rhyme was polished once too often,
And all the loving princes sailed away.

The happiest life among a thousand lifetimes
Finds me at sea prefiguring my course,
My weary friend is sleeping in the cabin,
I lie on deck at ease, my mind a stage

Where exits move toward doorways of farewell
Sweeping their plumed hats downward in an arc,
And unpredictable arrivals tread
The minuet that failed for all their Mozart.
Rock crystal yields to me the Vedic ruby,
The tall Plantagenet unseals my lips,
The mantel of Copernicus, embroidered
With dancing planets warms my lonely sun.
And evermore the breathing ship sails onward
Her helm lashed in the confidential wind,
The destination a surprise of daybreak
Not to be opened till I'm sound asleep.

There are degrees of darkness, there are shadows,
I can see something, someone at the helm,
But let my head fall back, and slip from Plato
To join a lovers' rowdy night in Athens.
The sea nymphs singing from the foundered island
Pursue my ship with melodies of foam,
And grim Odysseus grappling with his shackles
Thinks of his son grown alien with the years.
Weave once again, O sea nymphs, from the rainbow
Climbing across the sunny gauze of rain,
The rivers that meander through the meadows
Of all the earth to lose themselves in ocean.
Weave with your music the long summer twilights
When fireflies in the trellis wink and bloom,
The perfumes of invisible dominions
Of undergrowth outside the garden wall.
Sing how from embers of long burnt-out lovers
The bright Phœnician bird spreads out her sails
And bites into the waves with beak of bronze

Quelling them for the halcyon's flight tomorrow.
Always tomorrow calm will be the ocean,
The work accomplished and the song well sung;
The old Queen gropes along the path at nightfall
Through snow and cold and puts her curse on rhyme.

The little of the world I understand
Has come to meet me. We have gone full-circle;
Both empty-handed we confess that neither
Is richer for his circumnavigation.
The place we meet is in a leafless woodland
Dripping with autumn rain. We both had hoped
To meet some other character, some friend
In charity, who'd say: "I'll care for you
For ever; come, my house is up the hillside
Above the dank woods and the standing pools.
And here's an orthodox philosophy
To keep you warm, my grandma's famous patchwork:
Do take it, it will keep you snug as childhood,
Just pull it up above your ears and sleep."
But there we are, my shivering stock of knowledge
And I, the same as when we met before,
We turn our pockets inside out with laughter,
Then linking arms seek out the village tavern
And drink our wits away. Our argument:
That there should be a new tense given to syntax
Where present, past, and future all combine,
Then with such wealth of speculation, gather
Our nothingness together and depart.

I lie on deck, my hands behind my head,
And let the watches of the night go by;

The sloop is drifting with an oily motion
Smoother than wind as though the keel were drawn
But subtly-running underwater currents,
And all lies thick and quieted like chambers
Of human hearts when they have ceased to beat.

Wake up, you fool! I need you. Come below.

All right. There's no wind and there's not a star
To steer by if there were. What is it now?

What is it now? Look at the compass needle.
It's circling like the second hand of time,
Around, slowly around. Give it a knock.
No, it goes on revolving round the dial
Inexorably and steadily. It is
More frightening than speed. A compass, mind you!

Something to do with the eruption, maybe?
Some core of lodestone from magnetic earth
Bared by upheaval? Some electric chaos?
I am no scientist.

                    Around, around,
North, north by east, north-northeast, northeast
By north — it sucks my gaze around the dial
As though I had been drugged.

                              We'll wait for sunrise.
Meanwhile, I'll go on deck again to see
If I can find one star. No, no, not one.
And I begin to think there'll be no sunrise.

56

A strange and almost pleasant giddiness
Spins me. I feel that I am being unwound
From endless swathings of light gossamer.
Perhaps it was not, then, the compass needle
That was revolving, but the ship herself
Swirling like earth amid a noiseless maelstrom.
The dark is solid. Ah, no, not quite solid:
There are degrees of darkness, there are shadows
Deeper than other shadows. I see something.
Come up on deck! There's someone at the helm.

Who is it? Who is at the helm?

                    There's someone
Who knows these waters better than we do.
Now can you see him?

## A NOTE ON THE TYPE IN WHICH
### THIS BOOK IS SET

*The text of this book is set in* Estienne, *a Linotype face designed by George W. Jones, the eminent English printer, and named in honour of the Estienne family. The Estienne family flourished in France in the sixteenth century. Later descendants continued the family tradition for scholarship and fine printing.*

*This book was composed, printed, and bound by The Plimpton Press, Norwood, Massachusetts.*